THE FORSYTH GUIDE

TO

SUCCESSFUL DOG SHOWING

An informal photo of the most highly coveted award in dogdom—Best in Show at Westminster! Here Jane Forsyth, co-author of this book, gives the winner's smile to the Boxer bitch, Ch. Arriba's Prima Donna, at the Club's event in February 1970 held at New York's Madison Square Garden.

THE FORSYTH GUIDE TO
Successful Dog Showing

by ROBERT and JANE FORSYTH

Illustrated

Photographs by Evelyn Shafer

FIRST EDITION . . .   Fourth Printing

1976

HOWELL BOOK HOUSE INC.

730 FIFTH AVENUE

NEW YORK, N.Y. 10019

*To the many dogs
and their owners
who made it all possible.*

Contents

This book contains 91 photographs by Evelyn Shafer and five drawings by A Good Thing Inc.

"When You Buy a Dog," the AKC Dog Registration Application and Registration Certificate are reprinted in Chapter 1 by permission of the American Kennel Club.

Foreword

BOB and JANE FORSYTH are the best known and highly respected husband-wife team in handling and showing dogs.

They have made more champions, more group and Best-in-Show winners in *more* breeds than any other couple in the sport. For many hundreds of clients they have shown almost all of the 121 breeds recognized by the American Kennel Club. They have lost count of the number of champions they have handled to victory, but they now average about 100 a year. And both have shown dogs for over 30 years. In that span of time they estimate they have—together—won over 2,000 groups and at least 500 Bests in Show.

Jane began her self-supporting career in dogs at the tender age of thirteen as assistant to the manager of the Elblac Doberman Kennels in Massachusetts. She was a leading winner in Junior Show-manship and at age 16 she was winning groups and Best in Show. With a partner she started the Grayarlin Kennels for boarding, grooming and showing dogs in 1947 at Holliston, Mass.

Bob Forsyth was literally born into the dog fancy. His father was a professional handler and young Bob was working around the kennels when he was in knee pants. He became manager of the Seafren Kennels of Poodles and French Bulldogs when only 21 years old. In World War II he was First Lieutenant in the first combat platoon to go overseas with U.S. Marine Service dogs. He has received the "Fido" award as Best Handler of the Year three times. (Jane received the *Kennel Review* and "Fido" awards as Best Female Handler of the Year—each for three years.)

Both handlers have shown many of the top-winning dogs in America. Both have won Best in Show at the prestigious and highly competitive Westminster Kennel Club Show in New York: Jane with the Boxer bitch, Ch. Arriba's Prima Donna—Bob with the Whippet, Ch. Courtenay Fleetfoot of Pennyworth who became the first "triple crown" winner in history by adding to his New York win the Bests in Show at the International Kennel Club in Chicago and Harbor Cities Kennel Club in California in the same year. Jane also showed America's greatest winning Chow Chow, Ch. Ah-Sid's the Dilettante, to 96 group firsts and 26 Bests in Show. Bob has shown three of the four top-winning Old English Sheepdogs in history.

Their successes in the show ring are unequalled in the annals of the dog fancy. Their knowledge and expertise make them the ideal authorities to write the Guide to Successful Dog Showing. In this book they present, simply and clearly, their own winning techniques for the benefit of novice and experienced exhibitors alike.

The Forsyth instructions are enhanced herein by the how-to pictures taken exclusively for this guide by Evelyn Shafer, the world-renowned photographer of show and field dogs who has more than 57,000 pictures to her credit!

Bob, Jane and Evelyn hope their contributions will help to make better handlers and more successful winners of those to whom dog showing is the supreme sport and avocation. As their publisher, client and friend for many years, I know this desire will be fulfilled.

—*Elsworth Howell*

SOUND TEMPERAMENT

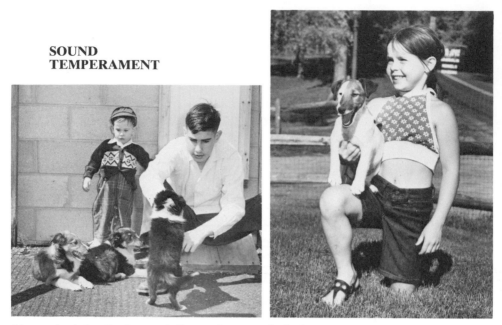

Always look for the happy, tail-wagging, people-loving, extroverted puppy.

Shun the shy, cowering puppy that will not come to you.

1

Choosing a Show Prospect

IN CHOOSING a show prospect much more is involved than visiting a kennel and picking out a dog you feel is a sure winner. Do you plan to show it yourself, and if so, have you chosen one of the heavily coated breeds that requires much care? Do you have the time, knowledge and skill to present your charge in proper condition? Or will you tire of the brushing and trimming? These are questions you must settle in your own mind. No one can do it for you.

Once you have decided on your breed, prepare yourself with as much knowledge as you can. *The Complete Dog Book* (the official publication of The American Kennel Club) not only provides you with the standards of all the breeds recognized by the American Kennel Club but also a short history which is important in understanding the reasons behind the physical structure and type of coat called for.

To most, the terminology used in the dog world can be quite bewildering at first. On receiving your *Complete Dog Book* we suggest you read the glossary.

Field Trips to Dog Shows

With a thorough understanding of the standard in your mind, field trips to dog shows are a must. There you can meet breeders and handlers with whom you may discuss points of interest that are not clear to you, while also compiling a list of people with young stock available for purchase. While watching the judging, try to evaluate the dogs. See how close you can come to the judge's placements. Bear in mind that this is not a true evaluation on your part since you cannot go over the dogs with your hands, and some faults are hidden from the eye. But you can see which animals have the right temperament, true tail carriage, good movement and overall outline.

The time has now come to go shopping. Make appointments to see as many prospects as possible, at the owners' convenience. This will give you time to evaluate and observe your possible purchase in its own surroundings.

Several very important factors are to be considered: age for one. Why? Because the older the puppy is, the more you will be able to tell about temperament. The young dog should have had all its shots, and been checked for parasites. Generally, the second (permanent) teeth come in from four to seven months of age. If overshot or undershot, and the latter is not called for in the standard, do not buy! If you are considering a male, be sure both testicles are in the scrotum. Ears if cropped should be standing. Lead breaking should have been started. One rule you must remember: the older a dog is, the less that can go wrong later.

Sound temperament is a must. Stay clear of a dog that shies away or cowers in fear after it has been around you for a while. Always look for the happy, tail-wagging, people-loving extrovert.

Coat is much more of a factor in some breeds than in others. Hard or wire-coated terriers for example must have a harsh wiry texture. Other breeds must be able to grow hair of considerable length. If possible, see the sire or dam, or both, if they are available, and check their coats. This will give you some indication as to the type and texture of coat you may expect their puppy to grow.

Is the color or coloring acceptable? It should be pleasing to the eye and conform to the breed standard.

Expression is determined by the size and shape of the head, the eye, the color of the eye, and placement of the eye and ears. You will notice that, with a flop of the ears either forward or backward, the expression can be completely changed from one of alertness

12

and fire to one of contentment, apprehensiveness, or even fear. If you happen to choose a breed with cropped ears be sure they stand up without aid and do not detract from the expression. If the ears require further care, ask to be shown what will be needed. If the trip is not too great, most breeders will be more than happy to recheck the ears for you later. This applies to breeds that may need their ears set.

Take enough time to have the dog moved for you several times. Don't let anyone tell you that this is just a puppy and is not lead broken yet, or that he is just too happy and is not moving quite right today. Insist that he be moved in the proper manner and under control. In most cases, a dog must be able to move with a full and graceful stride, the fore and hind legs moving parallel when seen from either end. Elbows should not be thrown out to the sides. Front feet should not paddle or make a circular movement, nor should they be pointing in or out. Rear legs should show a driving action when viewed from the side, with no sign of hocks snatching or turning out or in.

In the *Britannica World Dictionary* type is defined as an object representative of or embodying the characteristics of a class or group:

The head like a snake;

The neck like a drake;

The back like a beam;

The side like a bream;

The tail like a rat;

The feet like a cat.

This is an old description of the greyhound and a very clever one on type. Without these essential characteristics the greyhound becomes just another dog and unsuitable for showing or breeding. Type is probably the most important ingredient you must understand and find.

Outright Purchase, Co-ownership, Leasing

Once you have located a dog suitable to you, price must be discussed as in any other purchase. Has it been shown? If so what

WHEN YOU BUY A DOG that is represented as being eligible for registration with The American Kennel Club, you are entitled to receive an AKC application form properly filled out by the seller, which, when completed by you and submitted to AKC with the proper fee, will enable you to effect the registration of the dog. When the application has been processed in this office, you will receive an AKC registration certificate.

Under AKC rules, any person who sells dogs that he represents as AKC registrable, must maintain records that will make it possible for him to give full identifying information with every dog he delivers, even though AKC papers may not yet be available. DO NOT ACCEPT A PROMISE OF LATER IDENTIFI-CATION.

The Rules and Regulations of The American Kennel Club stipulate that whenever someone sells or delivers a dog that he says may be registered with AKC, he must identify the dog either by putting into the hands of the buyer a properly completed AKC registration appli-cation or by giving the buyer a bill of sale or a written statement, SIGNED BY THE SELLER, giving the dog's full breeding information as follows:

Breed, Sex and Color of the dog

Date of birth of the dog

Registered names of the dog's Sire and Dam

Name of its Breeder

Persons who purchase dogs that are rep-resented as being eligible for registration with The American Kennel Club and who encounter problems in acquiring the necessary registra-tion application forms should write to The American Kennel Club, 51 Madison Avenue, New York, New York 10010, giving all of the information they received at the time of pur-chase. The AKC will attempt to assist them in the matter.

THE AMERICAN KENNEL CLUB

owner of dog. Fee ($4.) must accompany application. Use this form for recording ORIGINAL transfer only

AKC DOG REGISTRATION APPLICATION
RETURN TO AKC IF NOT USED

	108

FEE $4.00
DO NOT SEND CASH
Add $1.00 For Each
Supplemental Transfer

DOG'S NAME ➔

1ST CHOICE

2ND CHOICE

The person who owns this dog and applies to register it has the right to name it. Limit name to 25 letters. Print one letter per box - skip a box between words. Names are subject to AKC approval. AKC may assign a number suffix.

BREED	LABRADOR RETRIEVER
SIRE	BUCKINGHAM'S BANDIT SA927543 (4-72)
DAM	SAM'S SUNSHINE SB 5983 (3-73)
BREEDER	SAM SMITH
LITTER OWNER	SAM SMITH 5229 MAIN ST DOLTON IL 60419

SEX **MALE**

DATE OF BIRTH **NOV 16 1974**

LITTER NUMBER **SL729497**

INDICATE DOG'S COLOR

Owner of Litter, circle the one letter below for the color which best describes this dog. If none apply enter color on last line.

A BLACK
B YELLOW
C CHOCOLATE
OTHER

JAN 15 1975
ISSUED

®The American Kennel
Club Inc. 1972

THE AKC RESERVES THE RIGHT TO CORRECT OR REVOKE ANY MISREPRESENTATION ON THIS APPLICATION IS USE FOR CANCELLATION AND MAY RESULT IN LOSS OF ALL AKC PRIVILEGES FOR THOSE INDIVIDUALS WHO VIOLATE THE INTEGRITY OF THIS APPLICATION.

SIGNATURE OF OWNER OF KENNEL NAME

I hereby give permission to use my AKC registered Kennel Name
IN NAMING
THIS DOG.

If you own a registered name prefix and are granting permission to use the prefix, complete this section. If your prefix is not registered, leave this section blank.

Person who registers dog has right to name it. Indicate TWO unique name choices. Choices may not contain a Roman or Arabic numeral; AKC reserves right to assign Roman numeral if necessary.

Litter owner should check sex specified on the face of the application, to be sure it corresponds to sex of dog being transferred.

Litter owner should indicate color by circling color that most closely resembles PRESENT color of dog.

Reverse side of blue application form. In buying a dog, do not accept an application that has not been properly completed in Section "A" by the litter owner.

INSTRUCTIONS: PLEASE TYPE – OR USE **PEN. NO PENCIL.** Erasures or Corrections may cause return of application for an explanation.

SEC. A MUST BE COMPLETED IN FULL and SIGNED BY OWNER OF LITTER (AND CO-OWNER, IF ANY) SHOWN ON REVERSE SIDE.

ONE box MUST BE checked
☒ I (we) still own this dog, and I (we) apply to The American Kennel Club to register it and have **ownership** recorded in my (our) name(s).

☐ I (we) certify that this dog was transferred DIRECTLY TO THE FOLLOWING PERSON(S) ON ___FEB___ ___4___ ___75___
                                                      mo.   day   year

MUST be filled in by owner(s) of Litter
PRINT NAME(S) OF PERSON(S) TO WHOM DOG WAS DIRECTLY TRANSFERRED ___MR. & MRS. JAMES JOHNSON___

ADDRESS ___631 HARRIS ST. LOUIS, MO 63120___

Signature ___Sam Smith___
      OWNER OF LITTER AT BIRTH   Signature   CO-OWNER (IF ANY) OF LITTER AT BIRTH

SEC. B TO BE COMPLETED and SIGNED BY THE PERSON(S) NAMED IN SEC. A ABOVE, PROVIDED the person(s) owns the dog at the time this application is submitted to the A.K.C. If the person(s) named in SEC. A has transferred the dog to another person(s). DO NOT COMPLETE SEC. B. Instead - obtain a Supplemental Transfer Statement form from the A.K.C. Instructions for its completion and use are on the form.

I apply to The American Kennel Club to have Registration Certificate for the dog issued in my/our name(s), and certify that I/we acquired it DIRECTLY from the person(s) who signed Sec. A above, and that I/we still own this dog. I agree to abide by American Kennel Club rules and regulations.

New Owner's Signature ___James Johnson___
                                        New Co-Owner's Signature ___Joan Johnson___

PRINT
Name ___James Johnson___   PRINT Name ___Joan Johnson___
Address ___631 Harris___   Address ___631 Harris___
City ___St. Louis___ State ___MO___ Zip ___63120___   City ___St. Louis___ State ___MO___ Zip ___63120___

FEE: $4.00 plus $1.00 for each additional transfer of dog represented by Supplemental Transfer Statement.
FEES SUBJECT TO CHANGE WITHOUT NOTICE

➤ REGISTRATION FEE MUST ACCOMPANY APPLICATION. MAKE your CHECKS, MONEY ORDERS PAYABLE TO THE AMERICAN KENNEL CLUB. DO NOT SEND STAMPS OR CASH.

When completed and submitted, this Application becomes the property of The American Kennel Club

Mail to: THE AMERICAN KENNEL CLUB, 51 Madison Avenue, New York, N. Y. 10010

Litter owner must complete Section "A" by indicating date of transfer and printing name and address of person(s) to whom he is directly transferring the dog.

If new owner named in Section "A" intends to keep dog and register it in his ownership, he should sign and complete Section "B". (Separate and individual signatures of all co-owners are required.)

Litter owner must sign Section "A" verifying details of transfer. Separate and individual signatures of ALL co-owners are required. Husband and wife must sign separately.

If the dog is to be transferred again do not complete Section "B".

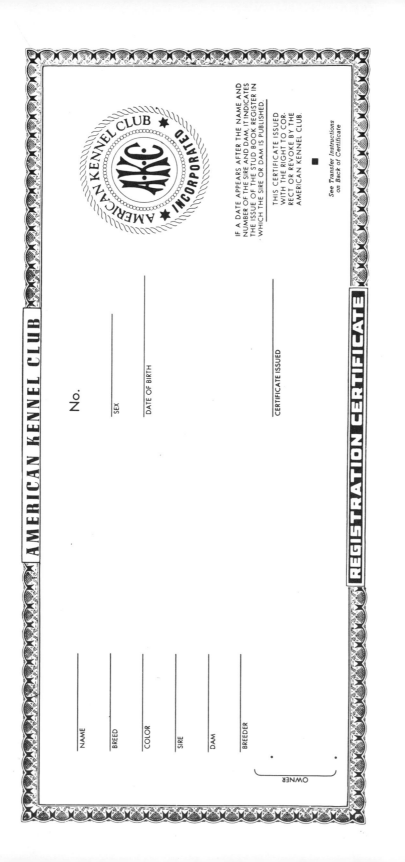

wins, if any, has it had? Naturally the price will be greater for a champion than for one not yet shown or shown sparingly. Age can also be a factor in price; the owner must recover the cost of raising a dog to maturity or near maturity. Many things may go wrong later with a young puppy that appears to be a sure winner.

Once a price you can afford is set, an outright purchase is best. If you cannot pay the full amount at once, a deposit is usually acceptable with a date agreed upon for the balance due. The dog usually stays with the seller with its board charged to the buyer if more than a few days are involved.

When making full payment, you should receive a pedigree and an AKC individual registration signed by the seller. If the registration is not available, the seller should guarantee in writing that it will be forwarded to you within a reasonable time.

If the owner refuses to sell you a dog outright, you may be able to work out either a co-ownership, or leasing, arrangement. Both require much thought, discussion and mutual agreement between the parties. Any such arrangement should be in writing and prepared by an attorney not previously known to either party.

The conditions of co-ownership may involve such items as some payment to the present owner; allocations of expenses like veterinary bills, show entry fees, handling fees and boarding; the sharing of profits from stud fees (if a male) or from puppies (if a female); the ownership of prizes; and the duration of the co-ownership (for the life of the dog, a certain number of years or other term).

The use of a professional handler may be helpful in co-ownership. Acting as a middleman or buffer between the owners, a handler usually cares for the dog, makes show entries, supervises breedings and serves as an advisor to both clients.

Leasing usually entails a payment to the owner for all rights to the dog for a specified period of time. All expenses are paid by the lessee and profits (if any) are retained by the lessee—unless the contract specifies otherwise. The ownership of the dog is transferred to the lessee's name and is so registered in the AKC records. In most cases the dog is returned to the lessor when the lease expires; this provision or any other disposition of the dog must be specified in the contract.

2

Train Yourself First

THE HANDLING of a dog is an art you can develop to a high degree, depending on your natural ability to have an animal respond to you under all circumstances.

It should be a bit easier for you, the owner-handler, to get this response since you are working only with one or two dogs at a time. With a little effort in understanding the basics of setting your dog up and moving him, you should become quite proficient.

Assuming you have attended a few dog shows, you have noticed certain individuals who seem always to have their dogs under control. Their work in stacking (posing) or moving their charges appears to be effortless. These are the people you must watch at every opportunity. Observe where they place their hands on the legs and the way they turn the head while in the process of getting their dog to stand in the proper manner. Do they leave the lead on or remove it while doing this?

In moving, you will notice that to acquire the desired effect, a handler will move with his dog and not require it to travel at an unusual speed.

When in the ring, learn when to allow your dog to relax while not allowing yourself this pleasure. The proper use of bait or a toy of some sort can be useful at this time.

19

Handling Classes

Handling classes to which you bring your dog can be of great assistance to you. They are run by many dog clubs and are generally open to anyone wishing to participate for a small entrance fee. The classes are normally run in a sequence of four to six evenings, once or twice a month, and are conducted by a professional handler or by an exhibitor with considerable experience. He is able to observe you in action. Here it is hoped your strong points can be improved and your faults corrected by personal instruction and suggestions.

If you are having a particular problem, discuss it with the instructor. He is better able to help you after observing you and your dog. For instance, your dog may be ill at ease, jumpy or nervous. Let the instructor decide whether your dog is nervous and high strung or if you are the one who is ill at ease and transmitting your nervousness to your dog.

Transmission

Transmission has much to do with dog handling and you will learn more about it as you gain more experience. The old saying, that an owner takes after his dog, really should be that a dog takes after his owner.

If possible, try to arrange for private instruction with someone who has the knowledge and ability to teach. And do not expect to absorb in six easy lessons all the knowledge your instructor has gained through years of trial and error, starting in much the same way as you.

Please do not confuse handling classes, where *you* are instructed in the way to *show* your dog, with obedience classes where you are taught to *train* your dog. To some degree, though, they will overlap.

3

Train Your Dog Next

A PUPPY coming from a show home or kennel has been handled from the time it was born. If handled properly, it should have gained confidence in human beings by the time it is able to walk.

If you have chosen an older unschooled dog which has just been allowed to grow up, you could be in for a problem. The older a dog becomes without some handling and training, the harder he finds it to adjust.

Table Training

When checking the teeth, a puppy should be put on a table. The same is true when cutting the nails, or for any other reason to examine the youngster. It should be placed upon a table with care to be sure that nothing is done to shake its confidence. An adjustable stand attached to the crate or table to hold a non-choke lead will prevent the dog from jumping off and injuring itself. And you will not only be table training but also teaching your dog to pose. In the show ring, toy dogs are usually posed on a table. And,

TABLE TRAINING quiets a dog and makes grooming, trimming, ear and teeth cleaning and nail-cutting easier to do. It also helps you to teach your dog how to stand properly for showing.

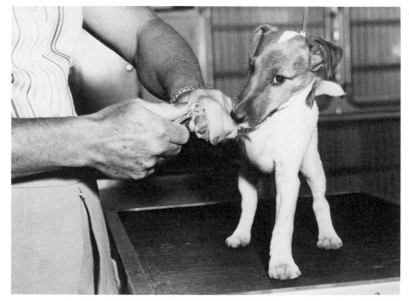

more and more, judges are using tables to examine smaller Terrier breeds.

Lead Breaking

When the puppy is eight or nine weeks old, use a leash while you move it from point to point. Realize that you are going to meet some resistance. With patience and understanding, gently pulling your dog in the direction you wish him to take, you will find your dog lead breaking more willingly later.

Your puppy must be treated with respect and affection but also with firmness. You must accept that he does not like the idea of a lead around his neck which prevents him from doing what he wants or going where he pleases, when he pleases. At this time a pat or two and a few kind words have a great calming effect. But you must be firm when leading the puppy from place to place.

Once your dog is used to a lead, you must lead break him properly. This can be done only by what is called a tight lead. A loose lead is great and looks very well from ringside but only after your dog has learned to keep his head up whatever the distraction. Control of your dog is done through the lead and not all dogs can be loose-lead broken. You must be sure the lead is as high underneath the throat, behind the ears, as possible. In this position you can keep the dog's head up where it should be. Walk your dog this way for ten or fifteen minutes. Of course he will object, but you must not give in. Repeat the same procedure the following day and your dog should be lead broken, at least to the point that he will go along with you even though not too happily at first. Walk him for ten minutes on lead, with his head up, giving him a few kind words and then having a game with him. Some respond to a ball, others to being pushed with your foot or to a light shove with your knee—play of any kind that your dog will enjoy for a few minutes.

After a few more minutes of walking properly, set him up. Don't worry if he is set wrong. Just be sure he stays where he is put. Ten minutes a day for two or three days and your dog should respect the lead and not object to authority. You may then try giving the lead a little slack, still keeping it up so that, if he tries to lower his head, move too fast or pull away, you still have control.

Do not overwork your dog. This is one of the most common mistakes made by the novice. Training should be done in the least possible time and with as little harassment as possible. And it

LEAD BREAKING—Resistance!

He's down!

He's up!

. . . but not away!

Time out for R & R.

All set now?

Up and away!

Good dog!

"Who, me?"

The Child-Dog Training Connection

Young dogs usually respond well to children who treat them kindly. Such contact enhances a puppy's adjustment to the training process and is recommended as an important step in broadening a puppy's environmental experience.

should never be repeated, unless your dog has a problem, and then work only on that problem.

Environmental Conditions

Your training sessions, when possible, should be held when your dog will be most comfortable. If you must work in the heat of the day during the summer, train him on grass. If you must work on black top or cement, be sure you have shade. In winter, do not work on snow or ice and when you can, try mid-day. Your dog will respond much more rapidly if he feels comfortable. If your dog is not responding, and you find yourself becoming overexcited, put him away until you are calmer. Only harm is done while schooling under stress.

Getting your dog out is a must. But out does not necessarily mean outside (which he should be as much as possible for exercise and development) but for adjusting to children if you have none in your household—possibly a young neighbor to play and go with for a walk. We have found that puppies and children respond much more rapidly to each other, making it easier for an adult to take over.

Pampering should never take place under any circumstance. Routine, kindness, firmness and common sense are the key words, if you wish to have a happy, well adjusted dog.

Once you have your puppy under control on lead, show him the outside world. Let him see and hear new things. If he is a little nervous at the start, a kind word or two will help him regain his composure.

A short walk close to an active highway, construction site, shopping mall or railroad will give him a great variety of sights, sounds and odors. If people stop to admire your friend and wish to pat him, let them do so.

Motion Sickness

Many young dogs are prone to motion sickness. It is wise to help them get over this as easly as possible. Put your crate with the dog in your car and go for a ride, being sure that he has not just been fed. Have paper in the crate to help in the cleaning that will surely need to be done when you return the first few times.

28

Motion sickness pills can be obtained through your veterinarian for bad cases, but we have not found them to be very effective. It is better to ride him as often as you can until he is used to it.

Keep in mind that a good show dog—in fact any good dog whether for show, field or companion—should first of all be a happy animal, and you must concern yourself with his happiness as much as possible.

To cure a puppy of motion sickness, place him in a crate and take him for rides in a car. Place newspaper on floor of crate and do not feed puppy in less than six hours before riding.

Lead in right hand, high on dog's neck behind ears.

Reach over with left hand to dog's left elbow to place foot.

4

Posing Your Dog

A GOOD DOG properly set up and posed is an impressive and a beautiful sight to see. To achieve this, you now have to teach your dog to pose perfectly and to stand motionless while the judge goes over him.

Start with the lead in the same position as in lead breaking, high up on the neck and behind the ears. Keeping the dog on your left side, grasp the collar with your right hand with the head at the proper level and reach over with your left hand to the dog's left elbow to place the foot in the desirable position. If your dog will not hold his foot where you wish it, take a firm hold of his muzzle with your right hand and gently turn his head to the right. You now have your dog slightly off balance and will find it much easier to place the left foot where you wish. As soon as the foot is firmly on the ground, return the head to its forward position. Replace your right hand on the collar with your left, place your right hand on the dog's right elbow and repeat, this time turning the head to the left with the left hand.

With your right hand again on the collar, run your left hand all the way down the back, while using the word "steady" or "stand" in a calm voice, so that your dog will understand that it is *you* touching him at the hind quarter and not something strange attacking him from the rear.

If dog moves foot out of position, grasp muzzle with right hand and turn his head to right. Then replace foot, and return head to forward position.

Switching lead from right hand to left, place right hand on dog's right elbow and set right foot, turning head to left.

Run left hand down back with command "steady" to left rear hock.

Hock in hand, set leg forward or backward to proper place.

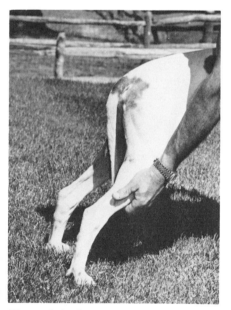

Place left hand midway on right hind leg and set right hind foot.

Bend hock to outside while setting foot so that hock faces rear.

Set tail to position appropriate for breed. Gentle rubbing under tail helps dog to raise tail to proper position.

To show correct topline and length and arch of neck, stand in front of dog and pull head up and forward.

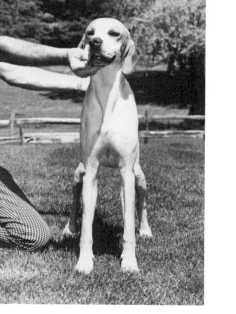

Front too narrow.

Front too wide.

Front set properly.

Hindquarter set properly.

Continue with your left hand running down the left rear leg until you reach the hock. With the hock in hand, now set the leg forward or backward to its proper place.

Still with your left hand, place it with the palm facing the rear in the area of the tibia or midway on the right hind leg and set the right hind foot. At this time you may bend the hock to the outside while setting the foot so that the hock faces to the rear. Recheck the left hock and foot and reset if needed.

With the rear in place, return to the front to be sure it is in order as your dog may move a front leg to maintain balance while you are setting the rear.

Your lead or collar still remaining your best control during this schooling, a sharp "steady" or "stand" given with a quick but not harsh snap on the lead will remind your friend who is boss and will not stand for any unruliness during working hours.

With your dog now four-square and your right hand on the collar again, place your left hand behind the ears, gently moving down the back to the tail. (Some breeds, such as Greyhounds, Great Danes, etc., do not require this step.) Set the tail to the position appropriate for your breed. For those breeds whose tails should be level or raised, a gentle rubbing under the tail or over the hip area will help the dog to respond by raising his tail to the desired position. Be sure to read your breed's standard for the description of the proper tail carriage.

For medium and large sized dogs required to have straight top-lines, it often helps if you push the stomach area up by hand. Or you can stand in front of your dog and, with hands around its head, pull the head up and forward; this technique is also useful to show length and arch of neck.

If your dog has been properly lead broken and handled at any early age, you should spend only a small part of your time in ring training for lead work or posing. What you do in ring training is to polish or remove the rough edges, with no more than thirty minutes in two days needed . . . unless you encounter a dog with a severe problem.

Once your dog has learned to be posed by hand, take him to a match show or two to be sure that he will respond under actual show conditions. If you find he is not as steady as when at home, give him a great deal of encouragement by playing with him, rubbing his ears, stroking him and talking to him quietly. But also correct him at the time. Be kind but firm. As in teaching a child, consistency is the name of the game.

NATURAL POSE

Using bait as instructed in text, and with lead if needed, train your dog to assume a natural pose or stance. In this picture the handler has bait in her pocket.

Hindquarter too far under dog. Hold lead under right ear and pull forward.

This action forces dog to move his front forward, thus extending hind-quarter.

Natural Stance

When your dog has become proficient on the lead, and while being posed, try to work him into a natural pose or stance. If you are fortunate, you may have one of those dogs that takes a great interest in everything that goes on around him. He may come to a well-posed halt, looking at something fascinating in the distance. No handler can ever make this dog look as magnificent as in this natural stance, but you can help.

Baiting

Have you taught your dog to bait, or play with a ball or squeaky toy? If so, you are one step ahead as, used properly, these are three of the most effective aids for this kind of schooling. The main object is to gain and hold your animal's attention for a period of time, while he stands free and four-square.

Toy dogs, Terriers and some smaller breeds in other groups, when on the ground or floor, are often shown in a natural stance without posing them by hand.

Most dogs seem to respond quickly to the offering of a special treat or tidbit, with ears up or forward, depending upon the breed, eyes bright and focused upon the hand that holds it. In dog show terms this is known as bait, carried in the pocket where it is readily accessible.

Many things can be used as bait, such as bits of chicken, steak or cheese. But liver has been found to be the best bait of all. Easier and cleaner to handle, prepared properly and kept in a tight container packed with salt, liver does not require refrigeration and keeps for a week or more even during hot weather.

Teach your dog to bait after he has been lead-trained and has learned to be set up by hand, when he will respond more quickly to baiting.

To work your dog into the correct pose, you must first gain his attention with the bait, improving his stance with proper use of the lead if necessary.

If your dog is inclined to stand with his hind quarter too far under himself, hold your lead loosely just under his right ear and gently pull forward. This puts him slightly off balance. He will resist with his hind legs and yet be forced to move his front to

While baiting, do not allow to sit.

—nor to dive for bait on ground.

Judge may ask that dog be stopped a few feet in front of him on return gaiting. Baiting into natural stance is shown here.

a more forward position, with his hind quarter in a more extended and proper stance.

Front legs are too wide? With your lead still under the right ear, pull gently to the right and forward so that you obtain a slight resistance in the animal's right side. Again off balance, he will have a tendency to bring his left leg underneath himself and both legs closer together. Use this technique too if your dog happens to stop with his front too narrow. He will then move one leg either to right or left to maintain his balance.

If your dog does not respond at first, do not become discouraged. Keep offering him a choice morsel from time to time, even at home, until he becomes used to accepting something from your hand. Baiting does not mean feeding your dog a meal. You want only to gain his attention, so give him just a small amount, holding the rest in your hand and tossing it into the air now and then so that he knows it is still there. If he becomes bored with this action, allow him a quick smell and give him another small amount. By varying this procedure you will be able to keep your dog alert for some time.

Do not allow or ask your dog to sit while receiving bait. Nor should you allow him to recover the bits from the floor. If you do, you will find him sitting in the ring while awaiting his reward or diving for bits of bait and even spots on the floor while in the process of moving.

If your dog refuses to bait or does so only occasionally, he may respond to a ball or toy that emits some sort of sound. This should be small enough to fit in your hand and pocket, in which it should be kept except when in use.

Balls and toys are used much the same way as liver. In fact, it is wise to learn to use them together.

The ball or toy may be thrown a short distance to gain the attention of your dog but should not be thrown so as to distract other dogs and exhibitors.

5

Gaiting Your Dog

THE MOVEMENT of your dog is important. But the way it is done in the ring, with ease and grace on the part of both handler and dog, is of equal importance.

Always keep your dog on your left side with lead in your left hand.

There are five patterns normally used by judges to inspect your dog's movement. The first, moving the class around the ring to check for soundness, is one in a counter clockwise manner with your dog on your left side.

You will find more dogs get out of control during this maneuver than in any other. So let your dog set the pace and adjust yours to his, allowing him to move out freely with a semi-loose lead to keep him under control.

If you are a novice at handling, we suggest you try to get yourself in the middle or end of your class so that you may observe others with more experience and also gain time to help your dog if he needs it.

The other four patterns are used for individual movement and any one of the four can be used singly, or in any combination if the judge desires. These patterns are simple, and require only that you observe the handlers in front to know which pattern the

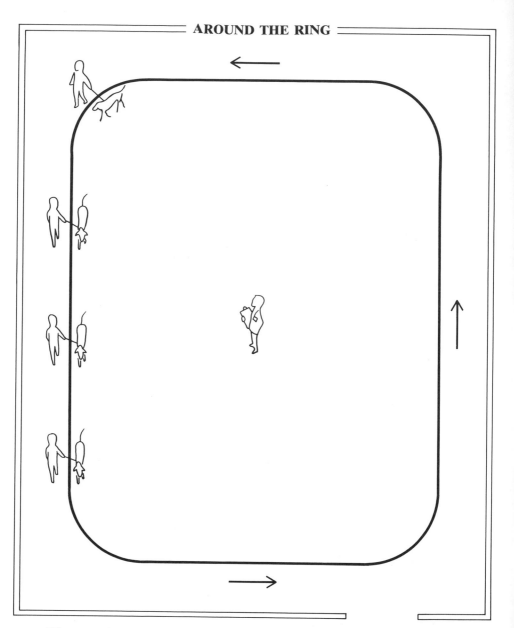

When a class enters the ring, the judge usually asks that all dogs be gaited around the ring together in counter clockwise direction. Keep your dog on your left side and leave ample space between dogs.

STRAIGHT OUT AND BACK

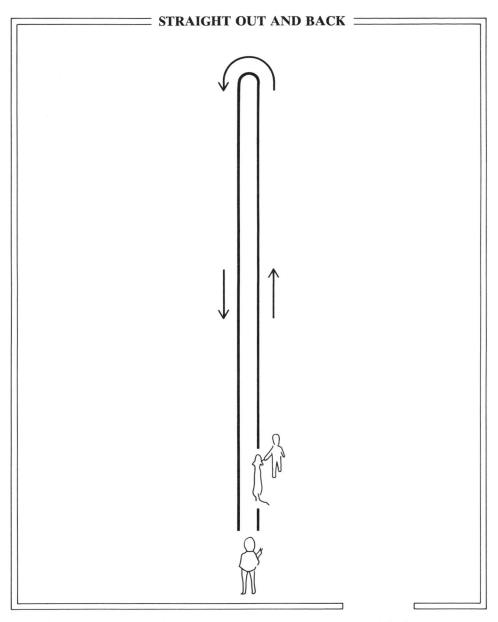

For individual gaiting, judges almost always ask for "Straight (or Down) and back." Start in front of the judge and move your dog in a straight line away from the judge to the other end or corner of the ring and return to the judge on the same line.

judge has requested. If you are the first to move, listen carefully to the judge's instruction and follow it accordingly.

Straight Out and Back

For instance, you are requested to move your dog straight out and back. Pick a spot in front of the judge in the direction in which he is facing and move your dog toward it in a straight line and with as tight a lead as required to keep your dog under control. Upon reaching the far side of the ring, turn and return directly toward the judge. You may be asked at this time to stop your dog a few feet short of the judge, at which point baiting, described in the previous chapter, comes into play.

The Triangle

The triangle—you again move directly away from the judge to the far side of the ring at which point you turn to the left at a 90° angle and proceed to the opposite corner, turning again to return to the judge.

The "L"

The "L"—move straight away from the judge and make a 90° turn to either right or left, depending on which side you have the most room to move. Upon reaching that point where you feel the judge has had sufficient time to observe your dog moving in profile, make a complete turn and retrace your steps in the form of the letter "L."

The "T"

The "T" differs slightly from the "L." Judges who request this usually stand in the center of the ring just off to one side. Here again you must move straight away to a point at the far side of the ring from the judge, make a 90° turn to your right and proceed to the right hand corner of the ring. Then make an about face and move your dog to the left ring corner. Again make a complete

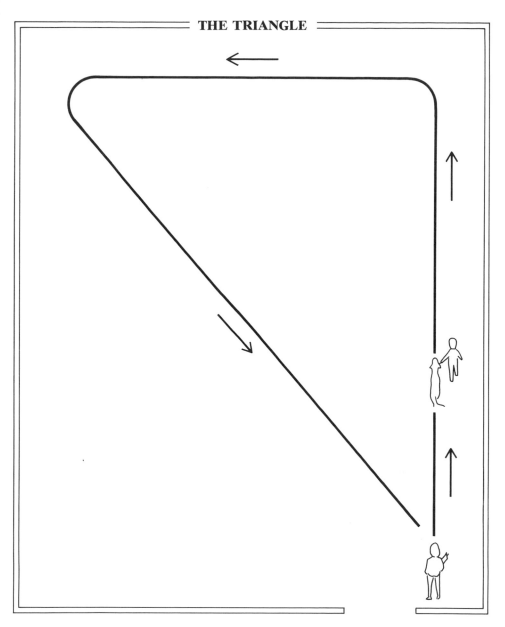

Move directly away from the judge to the other end of the ring, turn left at a 90° angle, go to the other corner, turn left and return to the judge.

THE "L"

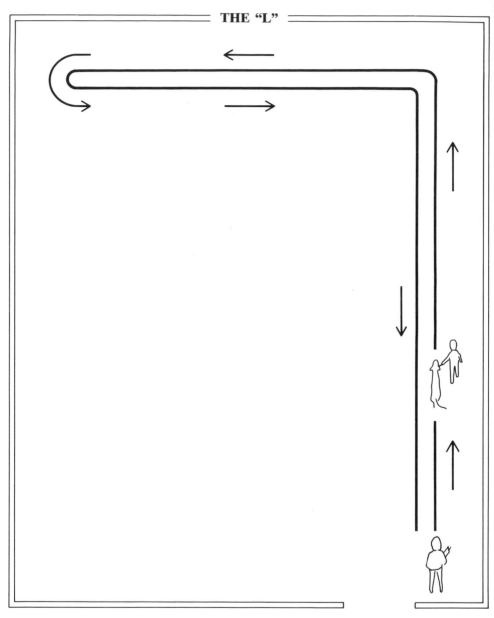

Move directly away from the judge to the other end of the ring, turn left or right—depending on which side of the ring you started—at a 90° angle, go to the other corner. make a complete turn and retrace your steps to the judge in the form of an "L."

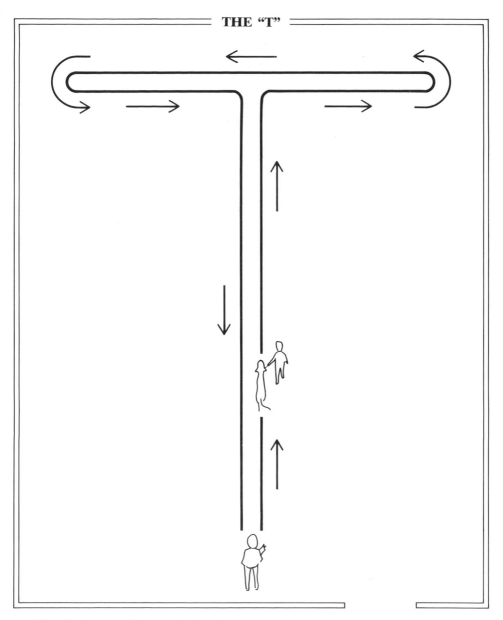

The judge usually stands in the center at one end of the ring. Move directly away to the center at the other end, turn right to the corner, make a full turn at the corner and move to the other corner. Turn back to the center and then move directly back to the judge.

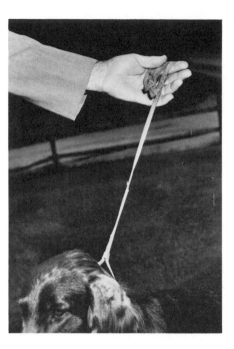

The proper way to fold excess lead in your palm.

COLLARS AND LEADS. From left to right: One piece slip lead; nylon choke attached to lead; flat collar and below it, metal choke; two piece nylon lead and choke; chain lead and leather choke and below, metal and nylon choke, and metal choke with long fabric lead.

turn back to center, turn 90° to your right and you should now be moving directly back to the judge.

Your dog should, of course, be kept between yourself and the judge as much as possible but not to the point of being detrimental to your dog's chances. If he does not move properly on your right side, allow him to remain on your left and work on this deficiency at a better time.

Fold any surplus length of your lead neatly in your left hand and move out smartly. Learn to work your lead much as a fly fisherman uses his line, playing it out and in with your hand as your dog moves away and closer to you in the normal course of movement.

Avoid moving too fast or too slow; neither presents a good picture. Letting your dog set his own pace is, as a rule, the best. In this way he will not be inclined to overreach himself or fall into such bad habits as pacing or ambling.

Collars and Leads

Your choice of the proper collar and lead are essential. The nylon or metal choke attached to a lead of moderate length is not only required to control some dogs but also looks better. Bolt snaps on leads for larger breeds are to be avoided because while running your hand up and down the lead as you are working your dog, it is very easy to release your dog unknowingly.

One piece slip leads, made out of leather and nylon, are very popular and can be used on all breeds. They are excellent for breeds in which the lead must be removed during posing. Whatever lead and collar you choose, it must be pliable and free from rough edges and metal parts that may become sharp while in use.

GROOMING AND TRIMMING EQUIPMENT

Each row from top to bottom—

First row: wire bristle brush, real bristle brush, wire bristle glove, real bristle glove.

Second row: slicker, palm brush, nail clipper, tooth scraper.

Third row: electric clipper, wide and narrow tooth comb, medium tooth comb, fine tooth comb, short tooth comb.

Fourth row: four kinds of stripping knives and razors, thinning shears, straight shears.

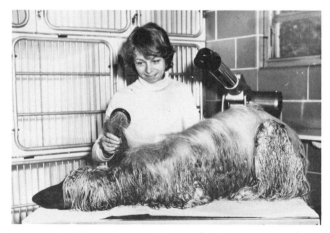

Long coated breeds may be washed once a week and brushed while using a dryer.

6

Getting Your Dog

Ready for the Show

PREPARING your dog for the ring is a constant, never-ending, but rewarding endeavor. Not only must he be trimmed and groomed to the best of your ability, but he must also be in peak physical condition at all times. A good animal, poorly groomed and conditioned, will have a low winning average.

Conditioning

Observe your dog to keep him in top bloom. His eyes should be clear and bright, his gums a good clear pink and his coat should carry a bright, sparkling shine. His hip bones should be covered, but you should be able to see or feel a slight indentation through the loin. His nose should be cool and moist. Internal and external parasites are a large concern and must be kept under control because nothing is more harmful to an otherwise healthy animal.

If undetected and not treated, a dog infested with these pests will, within a few days, turn from a clear eyed, lustrous coated,

51

BEFORE AND AFTER

An untrimmed, unbrushed Cocker Spaniel can look like this.

The same dog after bathing, trimming and grooming.

active animal to one that is watery eyed, dull coated and tires easily. It is advisable to have your dog checked for internal parasites at least twice a year by your veterinarian and treated under his directions.

Coat Care

Care of the coat must be done at least once a week. The frequency and time involved depend on the breed.

The smooth coated breeds require very little work: a good brushing with a soft brush, nails cut, ears and teeth cleaned (a must on all breeds), and a rub down first with your hand and then a damp towel.

If you have a smooth coated dog that carries a dense or heavy under coat, it is wise to remove as much dead coat as possible with a stripping tool or shedding blade. Holding the skin taut and your tool perpendicular to the body, move the tool in short strokes until all dead hair is removed. This is also to be done on longer coated dogs where the coat should lie flat to the body.

Long coats not requiring a hard texture may be washed once a week and brushed while using a dryer. Brushing a dirty coat produces snags that damage the hair. Refrain from over brushing. If done properly, once a week is sufficient, unless an emergency arises.

A long coated dog, whose hair should lie flat, should be bathed the day before a show and covered with a towel pinned in front of its chest and under its loins. Keep towel on the dog and the dog in its crate overnight.

Wiry or hard textured coats are not to be washed, except in areas of longer hair such as on the legs and whiskers. A cloth dampened with a cleaner may be used on the shorter haired sections. Brush vigorously with a stiff bristled brush. This may also be used on legs and whiskers.

Trimming

Learning to trim, unfortunately, is not easy. Not that it is hard to do, but it takes time and experience. The more often you practice, the more proficient you will become.

Contact the parent club of your breed and obtain any informa-

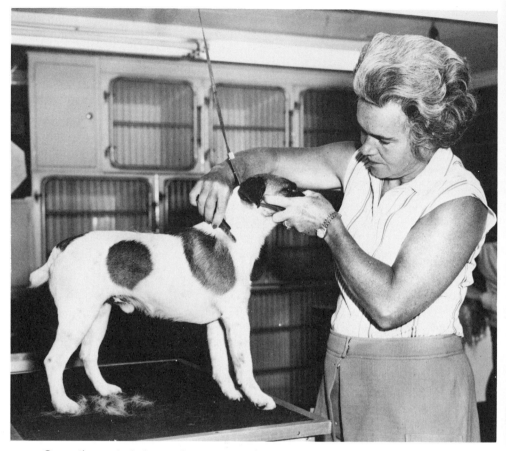

Smooth coated dogs often carry a heavy or dense under coat, especially around the neck. Dead under coat may be removed with a stripping knife or shedding blade. Note in photo above how much dead hair has been removed from Smooth Fox Terrier's neck by the accumulation appearing on table in front of its hind feet.

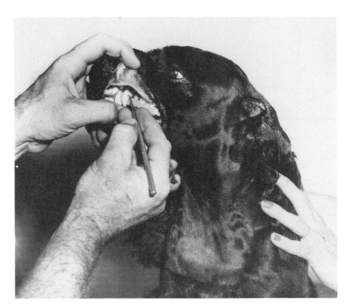

Cleaning teeth.

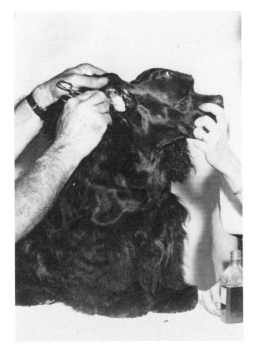

Cleaning ears.

Note mucus in dog's right eye. Clean eyes.

tion they may have on proper trimming. Read the books on your breed. Most contain a chapter with how-to-do-it illustrations on trimming and grooming.

Watch the owners and handlers of your breed as they prepare their entries for the ring. If they appear not to be rushed, talk to them as much as time permits. Then practice what they tell you and show you.

Learn how to use the tools required to do the job and when to use them.

Once you have your dog trimmed, let an expert review the result. Ask him to explain what you have done right and wrong; then practice. By learning various methods of trimming, you will eventually establish your own successful style and procedure.

Exercise

Overlooked by many, when preparing dogs for shows, is muscle development and tone. Whenever this is neglected, it must be corrected by proper exercise. The setting up of a run or paddock is ideal. The size of such an enclosure will vary, according to the size and number of dogs using it. Length is more desirable than width because it allows the confined animal to extend himself.

If the convenience of a paddock is not possible, walking at a good, brisk pace is excellent for both dog and owner. Having your dog trot beside you while you ride a bicycle, is also a good substitute. Larger dogs, if walked or run beside a bicycle, must do a minimum of five miles a day at least five days a week.

To obtain top prime condition, proper feeding and weight are most important.

Weight and Faults

Remember, proper weight, as a rule, is indicated by well-covered hip bones with a slight indentation through the loin. But there are certain breeds, like the Afghan Hound, whose standards call for prominent hip bones.

Other breed standards call for dogs and bitches to be over or under a certain weight. In such cases accurate scales should be used to determine the weight well in advance of a show. In this way, if a dog is a little under or over weight, diet can correct the problem.

EXERCISING FOR CONDITION

Long paddocks; car trailing and bike following at normal trotting speed.

Another, less common way of exercising a dog. Handler, horse and dog must be well trained to avoid accidents. Some dog fanciers object to the use of harness on dogs, believing it tends to impair action of forequarters.

FEEDING

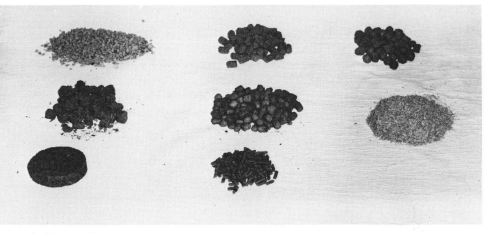

Left to right—

Top row: dry kibble small, to be mixed with meat and water; science diet, stress; science diet, maintenance.

Middle row: Prime; science diet, growth; wheat germ flakes.

Bottom row: burger, top choice.

Left to right—top row: canned food, ribbon type dry food, meal, kibble.
Bottom row: pellets, biscuits (two kinds.)

If your dog is short in neck, has a hole in shoulder, or is extremely short in loin or light in bone, show him on the lean side. The more weight a dog with any of these faults carries, the more obvious they will become.

With dogs lacking brisket, shallow in forechest or long in loin, present them a little on the heavier side—but not obese! Obesity is never attractive and, as in humans, is harmful to health and well being.

Feeding

Feeding should be done twice a day, preferably in a small, confined and quiet area. Allow the food to remain with the dog 30 minutes to an hour at which time any remaining should be removed.

A night feeder is not common. This is a dog that, kept in the same area with his food, will for some reason eat every morsel after confinement for the night.

A dry food mixed with beef and hot water has long been deemed the best all round diet by many dog authorities. Recently, though, completely prepared, ready to feed diet foods have become popular.

Whatever brand or type of food you choose to use, do not change it if it gives you good results. Constant diet change will only contribute to your dog becoming a poor and picky eater.

Your dog must be trimmed and groomed as close to perfection as possible *before* he goes to the show.

Leave as little to do at the show as you can. Who knows when your alarm clock will not ring or if you make the wrong turn or get a flat?

7

In the Show Ring

THE SHOW RING itself, of course, has been your goal from the start. Now you must decide in which class to enter and how. And what should you do at the show prior to entering the ring?

Regular classes at shows at which points can be awarded toward a championship under American Kennel Club rules are Puppy, Novice, Bred-by-Exhibitor, American-bred and Open.

To determine which class is best suited for your dog you should take age under consideration. If less than a year old, the best is the Puppy Class because he will be competing against dogs of the same age and stage of maturity.

There are cases in which a dog, particularly in smaller breeds, is mature beyond his age. In this case he may be entered in one of the other classes for which he is eligible, remembering that he must not only be as mature as his competition but also as ring wise and well conditioned as the older dogs are.

You may enter in the Puppy Class if your dog is at least six months of age and under twelve, whelped in the United States or Canada and is not a champion of record.

The Novice Class, one step above Puppy, allows you to enter if six months of age or over, whelped in the United States or Canada, but only if, prior to the closing date for your entry, the dog has not won three first awards in the Novice Class, nor a first prize in Bred-by-Exhibitor, American-bred or Open Classes, nor been awarded points at another show.

Novice is another fine class for the inexperienced young dog and handler because you will usually find few professionals or experienced breeder-owners in it.

To enter the Bred-by-Exhibitor Class your dog must be over six months of age, whelped in the United States and not a champion, owned wholly or in part by the person or the spouse of the person who was the breeder or one of the breeders of record. If bred in Canada, the dog must be registered individually with the American Kennel Club. The dogs in this class must be handled by the owner or by a member of the immediate family. The American Kennel Club has defined immediate family for this purpose as: husband, wife, father, mother, son, daughter, brother, sister.

The American-bred Class is open to all non-champion dogs six months of age or over, bred and whelped in the United States.

The Open Class is for any dog over six months of age, except in a member specialty club show held only for American-bred dogs. This being the most widely used of all the classes, we suggest that the novice exhibitor-handler start cut in one of the smaller, less used classes until he has a better understanding of what is happening and why.

Starting out in the Puppy Class and working gradually up the ladder to the Open Class will give you an excellent opportunity to observe not only your dog's development but will help you develop what is called "an eye for a good dog."

Any of the following breed magazines will give a list of forthcoming shows, their dates and locations and the Superintendent or Show Secretary to whom you may write for further information and official entry forms on which all entries must be made:

Pure-bred Dogs—American Kennel Gazette, 51 Madison Ave., New York, N.Y. 10010

Popular Dogs, Suite 1500, One Park Ave., New York, N.Y. 10016

Dog World Magazine, 10060 West Roosevelt Rd., Westchester, Ill. 60153

National Dog, P.O. Box 758, Palos Verdes Estates, Ca. 90274

Exercise pen.

In the ring avoid facing down hill with any breed having a level or sloping top line. The boxer here is standing down hill causing her to brace in front and to show a poor top line.

Care at the Show

Upon arrival on the show grounds, after unloading your crate and equipment, be sure to exercise your friend in the pens provided and give him a drink of water. Riding, even for experienced dogs, creates excitement, and he will require more water while travelling.

If your dog refuses to use the exercise pen, the use of a suppository for the first few shows will teach him to relieve himself in the proper place, saving you possible embarrassment in the ring.

Once the necessities are taken care of, examine your dog for cleanliness and any last minute trimming or brushing that may be necessary. Then let him relax while you check out your ring before your class is called.

What to Look For in the Ring

If the ring is outdoors and is uneven or not level, find the spot where you think your dog will look its best. Avoid facing down hill with a breed whose standard calls for a level or sloping top line, though this can be of some advantage to a breed required to be higher at the croup.

When you see what your ring is like, watch the judge as he goes over and moves at least two dogs. In this way you will know which pattern he prefers in movement and whether he examines every dog in the class individually and then moves them, or moves each dog as soon as examined.

If you are the first exhibitor to enter the ring, choose the spot which is best for you and set your dog up. If you are first in a large class, remember you must set up in the far corner to allow room for the dogs behind you. You may be defeating your purpose if there is a higher point or roll in the middle of the ring; in this case you may be better off in the middle or end of the class.

Check for holes or uneven spots that could throw you, your dog, or both of you off stride.

Always know where the judge is and what he is doing. Keep your dog relaxed but never get caught off guard.

The Judge's Procedure and Following It

The judge is examining and moving the dog in front of you; move your dog and set him up in the same area that the dog or handler in front of you has just vacated. If every dog in the class

FINISHING TOUCHES

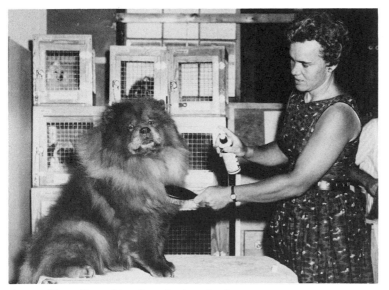

Jane Forsyth adds the last minute brushup to the Chow Chow, Ch. Ah-Sid's the Dilettante.

Bob Forsyth does the same for one of the Best-in-Show Old English Sheepdogs.

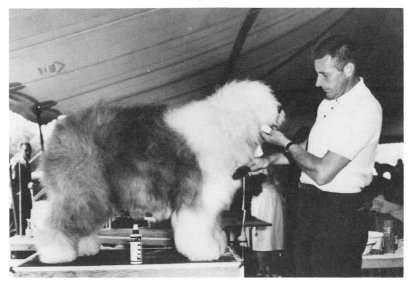

is being examined prior to moving any of them, set yours up when the judge is two dogs ahead of you.

To begin examination of your dog, the judge will usually approach its front. If your dog is medium to large in size, you should move to its rear, both to give the judge room and freedom to check the front and to give you a chance to double-check the hindquarter stance. As the judge leaves the front of your dog, you should move to the front and hold your dog's head while the judge examines the hindquarter. Be prepared to reset any leg the dog moves out of line, but do not reset a leg at the same time the judge is resetting another leg. And never get in the judge's way.

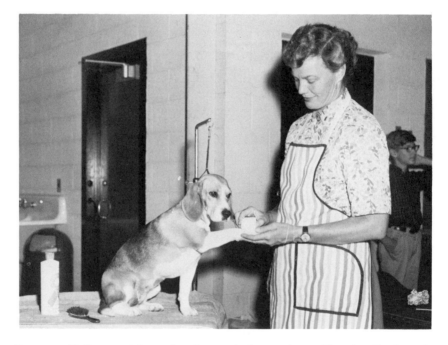

Damara Bolte applying cleaning substance to a Beagle. Such substances must be removed before entering the ring.

8

Dog Show Etiquette

LIKE GOLF, dog shows are a gentlemen's sport. Good manners, coupled with proper dress and courtesy, will enhance the picture you wish to present. Upon entering the show ring, the first impression a judge receives will be of you. And it means a great deal.

Dressing for Shows

Dressing for shows is not always as easy as it sounds, particularly if outdooors in areas subject to quick changes in temperature. Always wear something comfortable for the day's weather. Keep rain gear and a warm jacket or sweater in your car for sudden changes.

Foot wear should be comfortable and serviceable. Leather heels and soles are inclined to be slippery and so we advise walking shoes with crepe or rubber soles to prevent the embarrassment and possible injury of a fall.

Jangling, noisy jewelry of any kind should never be worn while in the show ring. It may not only disturb your own dog at the wrong moment but it also distracts the others and gets in the way of an otherwise fine handling performance.

How NOT to Dress for Showing a Dog

This informal costume is in bad taste. And sandals make for unsafe footing.

A mini skirt is a no-no too. Platform shoes are dangerous for gaiting a dog anywhere.

Too dressy! Shawls, pompons, dangling jewelry—any items that impede handling or get in the dog's way—should not be worn. And note spiked shoes!

AN IDEAL DOG-SHOWING COSTUME

Here is an attractive, functional dress with a gored skirt for freedom of action and a deep side pocket to hold bait, a comb or brush. Note sensible and comfortable shoes with ridged rubber soles.

Dress for freedom of movement and good taste. Tight clothes restrict your flexibility and loose fitting garb may flap annoyingly in your dog's face or hinder the judge's examination. It could mean the difference between winning and losing.

Men's clothes have a distinct advantage with pockets in which to carry bait, comb, brush or other paraphernalia required to touch up your dog in the ring. Ladies must buy show outfits with pockets, or have them put in. An alternative is to have a small pouch made that can be attached to a belt or to the clothing with a safety pin.

A jacket, with a neat shirt and tie or sport shirt, is normally worn by a man in the ring. Jackets may be dispensed with during periods of hot weather.

When choosing your wardrobe, try to avoid material and dark colors that show white hair and paw prints from dust, etc. Color of clothing is important. Colors may complement your dog but not at the risk of having the color of your dog blend into a similar color in your clothes. Wear lighter colors for a black or dark colored dog, and darker colors for a white or lightly colored dog.

Report to the steward any absentee you may have well in advance of the class.

Ask the ring steward for your numbered arm band at least one class prior to yours and be at ringside on time to enter when your class is called. Being late not only holds up the judge, who is on a time schedule, but also others in the class who may have another dog to do up or another class to enter. Wear your arm band on your left upper arm and place it so the judge and steward can see its number.

Good taste is not exhibited in dress alone. It should be coupled with courtesy. Together the two will leave a lasting impression and will help you in your entire show career.

Positioning Your Dog

On entering a ring, always allow sufficient distance between your dog and others. It is not necessary to crowd or interfere with other entries.

If you are first in line, you can and should expect others to set up directly behind you in a straight line. If someone else is in front, you should adhere to the same policy.

In other words, do unto others as you would have them do unto you. Comply with a judge's wishes, even though you may see no

This picture shows proper distance between dogs. Note also the proper attire of the first two gentlemen with neat shirts, ties, jackets and trousers. The man on the right forgot his tie!

Showing dog's bite to judge.

Judge examining dog's bite.

It is bad form to stare at the judge.
The best handlers avoid it.

reason for them. He must have his reason or he would not make the request.

We have always found that, if a judge thinks you have the best dog, he will find you. There is no need to force your way to the front.

Courtesy to the Judge

The judge may open your dog's mouth to examine its teeth. Or he may ask you to do so. You will, of course, have trained your dog to permit anyone to open its mouth.

If you are showing a bitch in season, the judge will appreciate your telling him so before he reaches her hind quarter in his examination.

Whenever you receive an award, be it Best in Show or fourth in a puppy class, a "thank you" and a smile when you receive your ribbon do not hurt, even if you disagree.

Remain at ringside with your dog if you have gone second in any class. You never know when the dog that defeated yours may go Winners requiring you to return for the judging of Reserve Winners.

Do not detain a judge after your class to discuss the merits of your entry or to ask why he placed the class as he did. Wait until he is through judging and leaves the ring.

Photographs

If you want a picture to remind you of a particular win, ask the steward if the judge has time to have one taken. If so, ask the steward to have a photographer paged. There are times when you will receive a refusal. You must then wait until it is more convenient for the judge.

Never approach a judge with animosity or display a fit of anger, leaving yourself open for disciplinary action. After all, you asked for the judge's opinion when you made your entry and you should accept his decision with grace.

Keep your dog on a short lead while in the confined areas of the crates and rings. Even though yours may not be aggressive, other dogs are. There have been cases of serious injury because some people have been careless and inattentive.

Cooperation

In most events where many people are involved, little annoyances may crop up at the time. Later they may be dealt with easily by a little cooperation and consideration.

Club officials and superintendents have a large responsibility in seeing that shows are run on time and as smoothly as possible. Without your help, this would be an impossible and aggravating task.

Cooperation, given quickly, with any reasonable request facilitates matters considerably and makes your day more enjoyable.

If you know of any problem with your entry, discuss it with the superintendent before you are due in the ring. He can tell you what can or cannot be done. Take care of this so that it does not impede judging.

Protests

Protests from other exhibitors against dogs are allowable under rules applying to dog shows either through the judges, verbally, under certain conditions, or in writing through the superintendent in other cases.

Protests at times are warranted and should be made, but in most cases they should be left to the judge.

If you do feel that you must make a protest, be sure that you know the Rules Applying to Registration and Dog Shows. They can be obtained on request, free of charge, from The American Kennel Club and should be on your required reading list.

Keep your dog on a short lead at shows.

9

Improve Your

Winning Average

A GOOD DOG will, if in condition and handled reasonably well, find his own winning level. This statement has been made many times and it is true. But a good dog can be helped to a degree by the person on the end of the lead.

We know a dog will no longer improve physically once he has reached maturity. So we must improve on the handler's ability to present the best picture.

Overtraining

We believe that once a dog has been taught to lead and set up properly, there is no need to rehearse him at it every two or three days, or even the day before a show.

To do so is to push him to a point of boredom, which may never be overcome.

Most novices fail to realize that they are asking show dogs to do something that is not normal or natural for them.

On a hot day your dog will appreciate sitting in your shadow in the ring when not under examination.

Dogs were bred to enjoy hunting, herding cattle, protecting their masters and their property, or just lying at their feet.

Tension and Relaxation

Although you can train your dog to stand immobile for long periods of time and to move the way you wish on a lead, you must keep him happy and make him believe he is enjoying it.

Stage fright or nerves must be avoided at all costs. Animals seem to sense this and will not perform well with a nervous person at the other end of the lead.

You can help yourself, and your dog, in this regard by getting him to respond to some sort of play when not under the eye of the judge.

If in a large class, allow him to lie down if he wants to. Just be sure he is on his feet in time to be presented to the judge.

Never expect to receive more from your dog than you are willing to put out.

Confidence

The desire to win must never be overlooked by any person who is engaged in a competitive sport. But we must remember that on any given day a competitor may be as good, if not better, than you are.

When you enter the ring, you must mentally condition yourself to win whatever odds you believe may be encountered. In this way, you always perform at the peak of your ability.

That does not mean you must become overly aggressive. There is a difference between being confident and being combative.

Comfort of Your Dog

Your dog's welfare must always be on your mind, even in the ring. If the day is hot and sunny, find a spot of shade. If nothing else is available, use your shadow for his comfort.

Always keep him as dry and warm as you can.

These things may seem quite small and unimportant in some respects. But the little things often give you the edge when it counts.

Throaty dog. See below for corrections.

Grasp loose skin and hold it at back of dog's under jaw.

Using lead, pull loose skin tight against dog's neck.

10

Unusual Show Conditions

UNFORTUNATELY dog shows cannot always be held under the most favorable conditions. Poor weather, noises, slippery surfaces, etc. must be coped with, as quickly as possible, to increase your chances of winning.

Weather, particularly at outdoor shows, can present some seemingly insurmountable problems, but with a little thought, care and work many of them can be eliminated.

Cold, Wetness and Heat

Always keep your dog warm, dry and free from draft for better performance.

Those with a smooth coated breed must pay particular attention to warmth. Keep a towel over a short coated dog when he is being worked on, or when taken to or from the ring. You may also give him the benefit of a towel in large classes while not under observation.

A toy dog can be held in your arms under your sweater or jacket where it can also benefit from your body heat.

Rain will make any dog uncomfortable, and long haired breeds

COLD AND HEAT PROTECTION

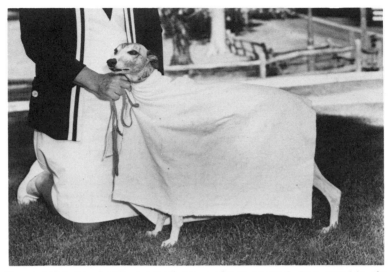

On a cold day keep a towel on a short coated dog outside the ring and even inside the ring when dog is not under observation. On a hot day use dampened towel.

Small dog can be kept warm under your sweater or jacket.

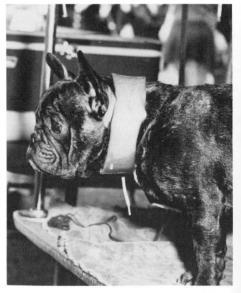

Ice collar on neck or ice bag held to stomach keeps dog cool.

FOR SLIPPERY FOOTING

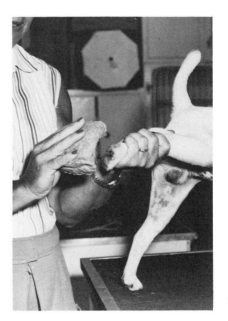

Wipe rear pads with damp sponge.

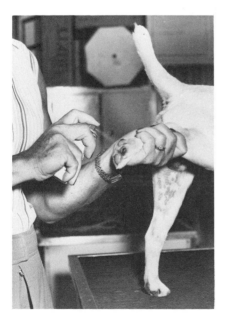

Or use non-slip spray product available at pet suppliers.

will be unsightly as well. Here again a towel or rain jacket thrown over the dog will help. Carry him over wet areas, if possible.

For emergency drying purposes, towel dry as best you can, apply corn starch liberally and brush thoroughly. Repeat corn starch as often as necessary. Be sure you remove all corn starch because such cleaning or drying substances must be removed before the dog enters the ring.

Heat can be extremely hard on a dog. A cool damp towel draped over a smooth coated dog or an ice bag held to the stomach area of any breed helps to cool it.

Avoid keeping your dog in air-conditioning. We have found dogs so kept show signs of stress much more rapidly when exposed to heat.

Footing

At times you will have trouble in setting your dog up, due to slippery footing. This can happen not only on floors or mats but on dry short grass. Wipe the pads with a damp sponge, or use non-slip products available from dog equipment suppliers at the show and easily carried in your pocket ready to apply when needed.

Sudden noises can be distracting, and much more so to a young dog since he will not recover as quickly. Reassure your charge by hand and voice. Allow him to look in the direction from which the noise came to reassure himself. Help him regain his confidence and composure as quickly as you can, and return to the job at hand.

Be on the alert at all times when in a crowded ring. If your dog is on the aggressive side, keep him away from others.

Always be sure you know where the other handlers and their dogs are in relation to your own position.

Wet or short dry grass and mats or floors indoors can make footing hazardous for you and your dog. When on such surfaces, do not stop too short or take corners too sharp or fast. Care must be taken, not only to prevent injury but to avoid sending your friend into a panic.

Females in season are allowed to be shown and can create havoc in classes in which both sexes are eligible to compete. The handler of such an entry should allow the males to enter the ring first. If the judge asks you to position yourself in front of a male, inform

BENCHED SHOWS

A benched show scene. Some exhibitors place their dogs in wire crates that fit within the benches.

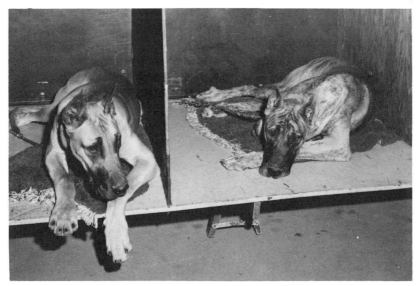

Dogs may be attached by short chain to their benches and provided with mats or rugs to lie on.

83

him of your charge's condition. Normally you will then be placed in an area that is less upsetting to the male entries.

Benched Shows

Benched shows are quite rare and present unique situations for dogs not experienced with them. Older dogs and youngsters alike can be upset upon finding themselves on a bench, and extra care must be taken to be sure that they are well watered and exercised.

If a bench chain is used, be sure it is not so short that the dog finds it hard to stand up or stretch out in the prone position. But it must not be so long as to enable him to get off. A leather choke collar is best used with the chain as it allows greater comfort and can not be slipped.

Open wire crates that fit the bench are the best answer for most breeds except the largest. Crates eliminate the shortcomings of the bench chain and afford more security for the enclosed animal.

11

Problem Dogs

SHOW DOGS must be taught. Some take to it rapidly and willingly, and others have problems or develop bad habits along the way. To cast the latter aside would be a waste of many a fine specimen that could be saved with proper correction.

Do not confuse fear with aloofness. Some breeds and individual dogs retain a standoffish attitude toward strangers, but do not display any sign of fear when approached. They are aloof but remain steadfast.

Fear

When approached by the judge, if the pupil of its eye becomes enlarged and its ears are laid back, your dog is afraid and is in or close to panic.

Corrective steps must be taken immediately. First, retain your own composure. Then a quick firm snap of the lead, and a sharp but quiet voice command of "steady," will calm your dog usually.

If the dog's fear persists, it may be advisable to place him in a different environment for a week or two where he will be exposed to as many strangers as possible. We have found this treatment works wonders.

Fear. Panic. Spookiness. May be caused by sudden noises or other disturbing distractions. It is advisable to accustom a show dog at home in advance to such distraction. For corrections in the ring, see text in this chapter.

Pacing

A very comfortable method of movement but awkward and undesirable in the show ring is *pacing*. This is a dog's gait when both front and hind leg on one side move in unison with feet striking the ground at the same time. Throwing the pacer off balance by a sideways tug of the lead or a push with the knee will put him back in a proper trot.

Sidewinding

The "sidewinder" can be a bit more difficult. Sidewinding or "crabbing" occurs when a dog moves at an angle to the straight line of movement. When gaiting your dog individually, instead of having him on your left, as normally, try moving him on your right. For some reason this seems to correct sidewinding.

If you feel unsure of yourself with your dog on the right side, vary your speed while keeping him on the left. You may find that you were setting a pace that was foreign to him, and he was trying to compensate.

If his head is to the left or outward of the line of travel, a good sharp tug or two on your lead will accomplish correction. This also helps to correct the puller.

Sitting

Some dogs have a tendency to sit whenever possible. There is no harm in this except when a dog is under the observation of the judge, at which time it must not be allowed. By placing your foot on the hind foot of the sitting offender, applying a little pressure and using the voice command of "stand," you will find your friend will soon associate the command with his foot being stepped on, at which point only verbal command will be needed. After a time or two, even this can be dispensed with.

Bracing

Bracing is a common problem you will face from time to time. It happens when your dog decides he is not going to distribute

SITTING AND BRACING CORRECTIONS

Place your foot on hind foot of sitter, apply light pressure and command dog to "stand!"

Dog is bracing so that front legs lean backward.

Gently pull tail which causes dog to restore balance properly.

JUMPING AND BARKING CORRECTIONS

Step gently on dog's hind foot.

Or bump dog's chest with knee.

To correct needless barking, use a water pistol or squirt gun filled with water and at the same time say "No!" or "Quiet!"

his weight evenly on all four legs. This, you understand, can happen in four directions: refusing to place weight on the left or right, or the front or back, although all four legs are on the ground. The wrong solution is to push, with the mistaken idea of forcing the dog to stand true on all legs. Instead, you must pull.

For example, if he has his weight on his hind quarter, giving himself a hobby horse appearance, gently pull his tail to the rear several times. This will throw him off balance enough to force equal weight distribution to the front. The same pull principle applied in the other areas should suffice.

Aggressiveness

Dogs being dogs, some become overly aggressive toward one another now and then. This is understandable, particularly in males, though some females have been known to show the same trait. However, aggression should always be under control at shows. If you have done your homework well and taught your dog the respect he should have for the lead and for you, there should be no difficulty.

Aggressiveness toward people can never be condoned for any reason and must be dealt with seriously.

Barking

Barking is one of the many ways dogs use to tell us something. They bark to go out, they bark to come in. They bark when they're happy, lonely, cold, hot, or visitors are near. And, like people, they bark sometimes just to hear themselves—which, sooner or later, will drive anyone out of his mind. A water pistol or squirt bottle filled with water and used at the same time as the command "no" or "quiet" will usually silence a barker.

If your dog barks while on lead, give a quick tug and use the voice command.

12

When a Little

Extra Counts

THE TIME will come when you and your dog will be pitted against an equal team for the big win. Then you must gain and hold the judge's attention—and even sway his thought, if possible, while he still has some doubt in his mind.

Do not panic. Keep your head and think. Quickly in your own mind, size up your opponent's dog. Does yours have a better head, front, top line, hind quarter or other point?

Once you have determined where your dog is better, work there. Without being overbearing, try to get the judge to concentrate on these areas.

Use your hands to present your case, without using them as a pointer.

Keep your eyes on the judge and know where he is at all times. But do not stare. Nothing looks worse.

Never overstress your point. Move your hand over or along side the head, the front, top line or hind quarter once or twice, no more.

Do not over handle.

If asked to move again, keep in mind your dog's best pace and

Handler on right is using his hand subtly to point out his dog's better front to the judge.

Showing the judge the better hind quarter on the dog at right.

move at that pace. Don't overdo it by trying to put on a show and moving too fast. If anything, move just a bit slower for better control.

If the judge asks you and the other handler to move both dogs together, get out first with your dog on the side he moves best, giving the other handler no choice. Do the same, if requested to set your dogs up side by side.

When moving together, you should set the pace. Don't be forced into moving too fast or too slow.

Take advantage of any mistake the other handler or his dog makes and make *your* move to give your dog the advantage.

Fulfillment of a dog fancier's fondest dream—Best in Show at Westminster! Here Bob Forsyth poses the winner, Ch. Courtenay Fleetfoot, the Whippet that won the honor there in 1964.

BIBLIOGRAPHY

ALL OWNERS of pure-bred dogs will benefit themselves and their dogs by enriching their knowledge of breeds and of canine care, training, breeding, psychology and other important aspects of dog management. The following list of books covers further reading recommended by judges, veterinarians, breeders, trainers and other authorities. Books may be obtained at the finer book stores and pet shops, or through Howell Book House Inc., publishers, New York, N.Y.

Breed Books

AFGHAN HOUND, Complete — *Miller & Gilbert*
AIREDALE, Complete — *Edwards*
ALASKAN MALAMUTE, Complete — *Riddle & Seely*
BASSET HOUND, Complete — *Braun*
BEAGLE, Complete — *Noted Authorities*
BOSTON TERRIER, Complete
  Denlinger and Braunstein
BOXER, Complete — *Denlinger*
BRITTANY SPANIEL, Complete — *Riddle*
BULLDOG, New Complete — *Hanes*
BULL TERRIER, New Complete — *Eberhard*
CAIRN TERRIER, Complete — *Marvin*
CHIHUAHUA, Complete — *Noted Authorities*
COLLIE, Complete — *Official Publication of the*
  Collie Club of America
DACHSHUND, The New — *Meistrell*
DOBERMAN PINSCHER, Complete
  Noted Authorities
ENGLISH SETTER, New Complete — *Tuck & Howell*
ENGLISH SPRINGER SPANIEL, New
  Goodall & Gasow
FOX TERRIER, New Complete — *Silvernail*
GERMAN SHEPHERD DOG, Complete — *Bennett*
GERMAN SHORTHAIRED POINTER, New — *Maxwell*
GOLDEN RETRIEVER, Complete — *Fischer*
GREAT DANE, New Complete — *Noted Authorities*
IRISH SETTER, New — *Thompson*
IRISH WOLFHOUND, Complete — *Starbuck*
KEESHOND, Complete — *Peterson*
LABRADOR RETRIEVER, Complete — *Warwick*
MINIATURE SCHNAUZER, Complete — *Eskrigge*
NEWFOUNDLAND, New Complete — *Chern*
NORWEGIAN ELKHOUND, New Complete — *Wallo*
OLD ENGLISH SHEEPDOG, Complete — *Mandeville*
PEKINGESE, Quigley Book of — *Quigley*
POMERANIAN, New Complete — *Ricketts*
POODLE, New Complete — *Hopkins & Irick*
POODLES IN PARTICULAR — *Rogers*
POODLE CLIPPING AND GROOMING BOOK,
  Complete — *Kalstone*
PUG, Complete — *Trullinger*
ST. BERNARD, New Complete
  Noted Authorities, rev. Raulston
SAMOYED, Complete — *Ward*
SCHIPPERKE, Offical Book of — *Root, Martin, Kent*
SCOTTISH TERRIER, Complete — *Marvin*
SHETLAND SHEEPDOG, New — *Riddle*
SHIH TZU, The (English) — *Dadds*
TERRIERS, The Book of All — *Marvin*
TOY DOGS, Kalstone Guide to Grooming All
  Kalstone
TOY DOGS, All About — *Ricketts*
WEST HIGHLAND WHITE TERRIER,
  Complete — *Marvin*
YORKSHIRE TERRIER, Complete
  Gordon & Bennett

Care and Training

DOG OBEDIENCE, Complete Book of
  Saunders
NOVICE, OPEN AND UTILITY COURSES — *Saunders*
DOG CARE AND TRAINING, Howell
  Book of — *Howell, Denlinger, Merrick*
DOG CARE AND TRAINING FOR BOYS
  AND GIRLS — *Saunders*
DOG TRAINING FOR KIDS — *Benjamin*
DOG TRAINING, Koehler Method of
  Koehler
GO FIND! Training Your Dog to Track
  Davis
GUARD DOG TRAINING, Koehler Method of
  Koehler
OPEN OBEDIENCE FOR RING, HOME
  AND FIELD, Koehler Method of — *Koehler*
SPANIELS FOR SPORT (English) — *Radcliffe*
STORY OF DOG OBEDIENCE — *Saunders*
SUCCESSFUL DOG TRAINING, The
  Pearsall Guide to — *Pearsall*
TRAINING THE RETRIEVER — *Kersley*
TRAINING YOUR DOG TO WIN
  OBEDIENCE TITLES — *Morsell*

Breeding

ART OF BREEDING BETTER DOGS, New
  Onstott
HOW TO BREED DOGS — *Whitney*
HOW PUPPIES ARE BORN — *Prine*
INHERITANCE OF COAT COLOR
  IN DOGS — *Little*

General

COMPLETE DOG BOOK, The
  Official Pub. of American Kennel Club
DOG IN ACTION, The — *Lyon*
DOG BEHAVIOR, New Knowledge of
  Pfaffenberger
DOG JUDGING, Nicholas Guide To
  Nicholas
DOG NUTRITION, Collins Guide to
  Collins
DOG OWNER'S HANDBOOK, The New
  Hajas & Sarkany
DOG PSYCHOLOGY — *Whitney*
DOG STANDARDS ILLUSTRATED
DOGSTEPS, Illustrated Gait at a
  Glance — *Elliott*
ENCYCLOPEDIA OF DOGS, International
  Dangerfield, Howell & Riddle
JUNIOR SHOWMANSHIP HANDBOOK
  Brown & Mason
SUCCESSFUL DOG SHOWING, Forsyth Guide to
  Forsyth
TRIM, GROOM AND SHOW YOUR DOG,
  How to — *Saunders*
WHY DOES YOUR DOG DO THAT?
  Bergman
OUR PUPPY'S BABY BOOK (blue or pink)